RECEIPE

From the kitchen of

Makes

O taste and see that the Lord is good. Psalm 34:8

RECIPE

From the kitchen of _____ Makes _____

_____

_____

_____

_____

_____

_____

_____

_____

_____

_____

_____

_____ *O taste and see that the Lord is good. Psalm 34:8*

RECIPE

Makes

O taste and see that the Lord is good. Psalm 34:8

RECIPE

From the kitchen of _____   Makes _____

_____

_____

_____

_____

_____

_____

_____

_____

_____

_____

_____

_____ *O taste and see that the Lord is good.* Psalm 34:8

RECIPE

Makes

O taste and see that the Lord is good. Psalm 34:8

RECIPE

Makes

O taste and see that the Lord is good. Psalm 34:8

RECIPE

Makes

O taste and see that the Lord is good. Psalm 34:8

RECICPE

Makes

O taste and see that the Lord is good. Psalm 34:8

RECIPE

Makes

O taste and see that the Lord is good. Psalm 34:8

RECIPE

From the kitchen of _____ Makes _____

_____

_____

_____

_____

_____

_____

_____

_____

_____

_____

_____

_____ *O taste and see that the Lord is good.* Psalm 34:8

RECIPE

From the kitchen of _____ Makes _____

_____

_____

_____

_____

_____

_____

_____

_____

_____

_____

_____

_____

_____

O taste and see that the Lord is good. Psalm 34:8

RECIPE

Makes

O taste and see that the Lord is good. Psalm 34:8

RECIPE

From the kitchen of _____ Makes _____

O taste and see that the Lord is good. Psalm 34:8

RECIPE

Makes

O taste and see that the Lord is good. Psalm 34:8

RECIPE

Makes

O taste and see that the Lord is good. Psalm 34:8

RECIPE

From the kitchen of _____ *Makes* _____

_____

_____

_____

_____

_____

_____

_____

_____

_____

_____

_____

O taste and see that the Lord is good. Psalm 34:8

RECIPE

From the kitchen of _____ Makes _____

_____
_____
_____
_____
_____
_____
_____
_____
_____
_____
_____
_____

_____ *O taste and see that the Lord is good.* Psalm 34:8

RECIPE

Makes

O taste and see that the Lord is good. Psalm 34:8

RECIPE

From the kitchen of _____ Makes _____

_____

_____

_____

_____

_____

_____

_____

_____

_____

_____

_____

_____ *O taste and see that the Lord is good. Psalm 34:8*

RECIPE

O taste and see that the Lord is good. Psalm 34:8

RECITE

Makes

O taste and see that the Lord is good. Psalm 34:8

RECECIPE

Makes

O taste and see that the Lord is good. Psalm 34:8

RECICE

Makes

O taste and see that the Lord is good. Psalm 34:8

RECIPE

Makes

O taste and see that the Lord is good. Psalm 34:8

RECIPE

Makes

O taste and see that the Lord is good. Psalm 34:8

RECIPE

From the kitchen of _____   Makes _____

_____

_____

_____

_____

_____

_____

_____

_____

_____

_____

_____

_____ *O taste and see that the Lord is good. Psalm 34:8*

RECITE

Makes

O taste and see that the Lord is good. Psalm 34:8

RECIPE

_____

_____

_____

_____

_____

_____

_____

_____

_____

_____

_____

————————————— *O taste and see that the Lord is good.* Psalm 34:8

RECIPE

From the kitchen of _____ Makes _____

_____

_____

_____

_____

_____

_____

_____

_____

_____

_____

_____

_____ *O taste and see that the Lord is good. Psalm 34:8*

RECITE

From the kitchen of   *Makes*

_____

_____

_____

_____

_____

_____

_____

_____

_____

_____

_____

_____

O taste and see that the Lord is good. Psalm 34:8

RECIPE

From the kitchen of _____ Makes _____

_____

_____

_____

_____

_____

_____

_____

_____

_____

_____

_____

O taste and see that the Lord is good. Psalm 34:8

RECIPE

Makes

O taste and see that the Lord is good. Psalm 34:8

RECIPE

O taste and see that the Lord is good. Psalm 34:8

RECIPE

Makes

O taste and see that the Lord is good. Psalm 34:8

RECIPE

O taste and see that the Lord is good. Psalm 34:8

RECIPE

Makes

O taste and see that the Lord is good. Psalm 34:8

RECIPE

O taste and see that the Lord is good. Psalm 34:8

RECITE

Makes

O taste and see that the Lord is good. Psalm 34:8

RECIPE

Makes

O taste and see that the Lord is good. Psalm 34:8

RECIPE

O taste and see that the Lord is good. Psalm 34:8

RECITE

Makes

O taste and see that the Lord is good. Psalm 34:8

RECEIPE

From the kitchen of   Makes

O taste and see that the Lord is good. Psalm 34:8

RECIPE

Makes

O taste and see that the Lord is good. Psalm 34:8

RECURRENCE

Makes

O taste and see that the Lord is good. Psalm 34:8

RECITE

Makes

O taste and see that the Lord is good. Psalm 34:8

RECIPE

Makes

_____

_____

_____

_____

_____

_____

_____

_____

_____

_____

_____

_____

_____

_____ *O taste and see that the Lord is good. Psalm 34:8*

RECIPE

Makes

O taste and see that the Lord is good. Psalm 34:8

RECIPE

O taste and see that the Lord is good. Psalm 34:8

RECIPE

Makes

O taste and see that the Lord is good. Psalm 34:8

RECIPE

_____

_____

_____

_____

_____

_____

_____

_____

_____

_____

_____

O taste and see that the Lord is good. Psalm 34:8